DATE DUE		
NOV 18 '86		

Decoupage
for young crafters

by Leslie Linsley   photographs by Jon Aron

E. P. Dutton   New York

For Lisa, Amy, and Robby

Text copyright © 1977 by Leslie Linsley
Photographs copyright © 1977 by Jon Aron

Library of Congress Cataloging in Publication Data

Linsley, Leslie   Decoupage for young crafters

SUMMARY: Instructions for decorating a shell necklace,
planter, pins and barrettes, boxes, and other things
with cutout paper designs.

1. Decoupage—Juvenile literature.   [1. Decoupage.
2. Handicraft]   I. Aron, Jon.   II. Title
TT870.L5414   745.54   76-53572   ISBN 0-525-28614-4

Published simultaneously in Canada by Clarke,
Irwin & Company Limited, Toronto and Vancouver

Editor: Susan Shapiro   Designer: Riki Levinson

Printed in the U.S.A.   First Edition
10 9 8 7 6 5 4 3 2 1

Contents

What Is Decoupage?

Decoupage means to decorate something with cutout paper designs. *Découpage* is the French word for "to cut out." Long ago artists cut out paper designs and glued them to furniture. The furniture was then lacquered to make it very smooth and shiny. The paper designs looked like they had been really painted on.

The projects shown in this book have been painted, pasted with cutout pictures, and then varnished for a shiny finish. You can cut out pictures from greeting cards, wrapping paper, and magazines. You can use photographs, postcards, baseball cards, even playing cards for decoration. Most of the things that are used can be found around your home. If you don't have all the materials to make a project, you can buy supplies in the five-and-ten or at a craft or hobby store.

All the children making craft projects in this book used *acrylic paint*. This paint can be washed off your hands and brush with water. It comes in tubes or jars. Other paint can be used if it, too, has a water base. While you work, you should always have a small cup of water and a paper towel nearby. A slightly damp sponge is also useful.

When you paint, dip the paintbrush halfway into the jar. Try not to get the paint all over the handle. If you use paint from a tube, squeeze a little onto a piece of scrap paper. Dip your brush into the paint on the paper. When you paint on metal, like a Band-Aid box, the paint takes a little longer to dry. After the first coat, wait 10 minutes and then put another layer of paint on the metal to be sure that it is well coated. Since paint does not last forever on a metal box, these projects will be fun to use for several months. After that, you can make something new to replace them.

To cut out the designs, use small scissors like cuticle or sewing scissors. Cut carefully around the outline of each design. Then glue the designs on the object. These crafters used Elmer's Glue-All or Sobo glue. Keep your sponge handy to pat away any extra glue that gets on your project or your hands while working.

After the designs are glued down, you should put varnish over the project to protect the finish and to keep the designs from peeling off. This will also make everything shiny. The *varnish* that the children used is *glossy polymer medium* and is made by Grumbacher, Liquitex, Weber, or Palmer. All art supply or craft stores sell one or more brands. The varnish can be washed off your hands with warm water. If you get some on your work table, wipe it up before it dries. If you get some on your clothes, you can wash it out. Best of all, it dries very quickly. So you will be able to use your project very soon after you make it. Waiting a long time for things to dry isn't much fun.

The children who made the craft projects in this book had a lot of fun and could make everything without any help from grown-ups. If you read the directions carefully, you won't need any help either. You can make a present for your mother or father or a friend and really surprise them.

Each project is rated *Easy*, *Medium*, and *Harder*. Choose a project best for you. All the projects can be done just the way they're shown here. Or you can create your own designs to change the project a bit.

Find a good place to work. Spread paper around in case you spill paint. If you wear a smock or old clothes, you won't have to worry about spills on yourself.

Caring for tools and materials is an important part of crafting. Clean your brushes in warm water after using them to paint or varnish. Throw out scraps and save extra material. Wipe up your work area with a damp sponge and put the tops back on all jars and tubes. A shoe box is good to hold supplies. Why not decoupage the shoe box!

Decoupage is easy. Once you learn how to do it, you can think up all kinds of things to make. Before you throw away a birthday card or an orange juice can, think about making something with it. You can become a recycler and learn a new craft at the same time.

Crayon Box

metal Band-Aid box (large size)
paint
paintbrush (½″ or ¾″)
small scissors
glue
picture from a greeting card
   or wrapping paper
varnish

A metal Band-Aid box is perfect for all your crayons. If you don't have an empty box, maybe you can find another container for the Band-Aids so you can begin your project right away.

A crayon box with your own design decoupaged on it will look nice on your desk at home or in school. If you don't like to color with crayons, a decorated box makes a wonderful marble holder. What else can you do with a Band-Aid box?

Douglas painted his crayon box red and decorated it with a colorful fish and flowers that he cut from wrapping paper. Maybe you'd like to decoupage yours with your name or a picture of your favorite animal.

Here's how to do it.

Pick out a color paint that you like. It should be acrylic so that you can wash it off your hands easily. Hold the box steady with one hand while you paint with the other.

Cover the whole box with the paint. Do not paint the bottom. Painting takes a lot of concentration. Don't let anything or anyone distract you. While Douglas was working, his little sister Rebecca kept making faces to get his attention. He just kept on working.

When you finish painting the outside of the box, leave the lid open so that the hinges dry and the lid will not stick closed. You can paint the inside of the lid if you want to.

Set the box aside to dry for 10 minutes. Don't touch it while it is drying. You can begin to cut out the design while you are waiting.

Choosing a design is lots of fun. Pick something that you really like. Be sure that it isn't too hard to cut out. Maybe you have a birthday card that a friend sent you. Or some wrapping paper that you saved. Find a pretty picture that is the right size for the box. Remember, the picture should fit on the front so you can see the whole design.

If you aren't sure of the size, here's what to do.

After the box is dry, lay the front down on top of the picture. If you can see the picture sticking out from under the box, the picture is too big.

When you find a design that is just right, cut it out with a small scissors. Cuticle scissors or small sewing scissors are the easiest to use. Maybe your mother will let you borrow hers if you are careful with them. Cut the picture out as neatly as you can. Take your time.

Check the box to see if it is covered with enough paint. Can you still see the words showing through the paint? If your box needs another coat, paint it the same way you did the first time. Let the box dry for another 10 minutes.

After you have cut out a design, turn it over. The picture is face down on your work table. Squirt a few drops of glue on the back of the cutout. With your finger spread the glue all over the back. Carefully lift the picture up by the edges. Place it on the front of the box.

3

Wet your sponge and squeeze all the water out of it. Press the sponge down on top of the picture. Gently wipe away any glue that is showing at the edges of the picture. If you want to, like Douglas, you can put more designs on the top and sides.

Wash your hands before you touch each new cutout so it won't stick to your fingers. Pat each picture gently in place. Be careful not to rip the design.

Wash your brush out in warm water until it is really clean. Squeeze the water out of the brush with a paper towel. Now you are ready to varnish.

4

The varnish will protect your box so that the paint won't chip. It will also keep the pictures from peeling off. Dip your brush in the varnish. Brush the varnish over the whole box with the lid open. If you put your hand inside the box, it is easier to do. You can also varnish the inside of the lid. The varnish will look white. The cloudy white color will disappear when the varnish dries. Put the box out of the way to dry for about 10 minutes.

If you want to, you can add two or three more coats of varnish to make the finish stronger and shinier.

Brush the varnish on all sides of the box each time you coat it.

Remember to let the box dry well each time before you put more varnish on it. The best way is to brush the varnish on before you go to bed. In the morning you can put on another coat of varnish before going to school. Then when you get home it will be perfectly dry.

Clean your brush in warm water so it is ready to use for your next project.

When Douglas was finishing his crayon box, Becky ran over to hug him. "Now it's my turn." 5

Shell Necklace

7 small shells
6 beads
wrapping paper with small designs
    or magazines
varnish
paintbrush (¼″)
ruler
small scissors
elastic string (20″ long)

Have you ever collected shells along the seashore? The inside of most shells is very smooth and just perfect for decoupage. When you walk on the beach, you can collect shells and small stones in a paper cup. Pick shells for your necklace that are almost the same size. Look for shells that have a tiny hole in the top. These are the ones to use for your necklace. Clean and dry all the shells that you want to use.

When you are ready to make your necklace, buy some beads at the five-and-ten or at a craft store.

You can do this project at a table or on the floor. Spread a piece of paper on your work space.

Samantha used wrapping paper for her designs. Use small scissors to cut out one small picture to fit each shell. If you don't have any wrapping paper, you can look through some magazines for pictures that you like.

Pick up one shell and varnish the inside with your brush. Place a cutout picture carefully on top of the varnish. Press the picture down inside the shell. Varnish the next shell and put a picture inside it. Do this so all the shells have a little picture inside.

Dip your brush into the varnish again and coat over each shell picture. This will make them shiny and keep the pictures from peeling off. Set all the shells out of the way to dry for about 10 minutes.

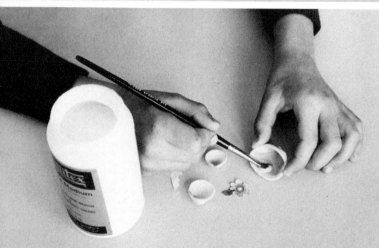

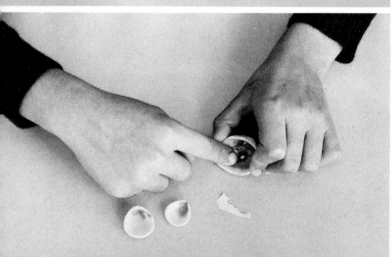

Take a piece of thin elastic string and use a ruler to measure 20 inches without stretching the string. Cut this piece off. When the shells are dry, you can begin to string them. First put one end of the string through the tiny hole of one shell. Center the shell on the string and tie a knot.

Next place a small bead on one end of the string and slide it down right next to the shell. Now put another shell on the string next to the bead. Tie a knot to hold this shell in place. String another bead, then a shell. Your necklace will have three shells and three beads on each side of the center shell. Tie the two ends of the string together and slip the necklace over your head, stretching the elastic at the back. That's all there is to it.

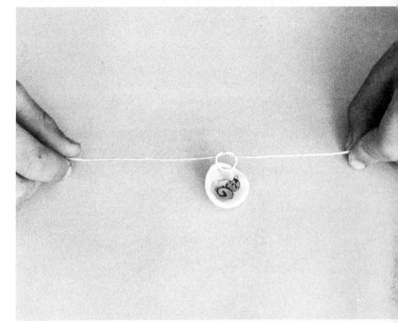

Douglas made his shell necklace with only one large shell. This was easier than making a necklace with seven shells. He is wearing the shell so that it is on top of the train on his sweater. That's the way he likes it.

Becky wanted to make one too. Since she is only four, she couldn't cut as well as Doug, who is almost seven. She painted her shell orange. Then she put a self-sticking valentine on it. She didn't have to cut anything out. Since she doesn't know how to tie a knot, she needed some help from Doug.

This is a good project for a little sister or brother who wants to work with you.

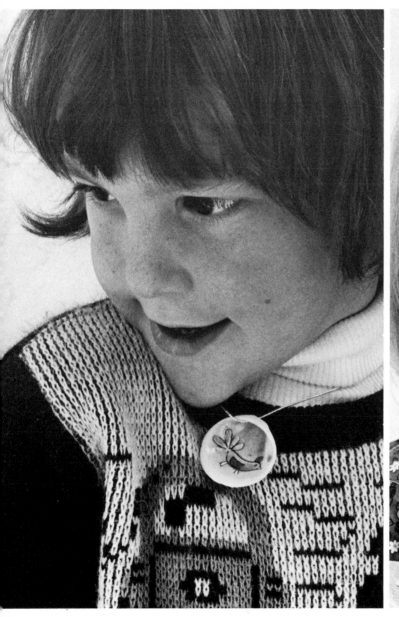

Planter

metal can
paint
paintbrush (½″ to 1″)
punch-out stickers
varnish
spoon
dirt *or* potting soil
seeds

Have you ever planted seeds? If you have, then you know how exciting it is to see the sprouts push through the dirt. Your very own planter can be decorated and placed on your windowsill. It will look nice when there is no plant in it and it will be even nicer when the plant begins to grow. A planter can be made from any size can, but the boys and girls in this third-grade class used small soup cans. Each child made a different planter.

13

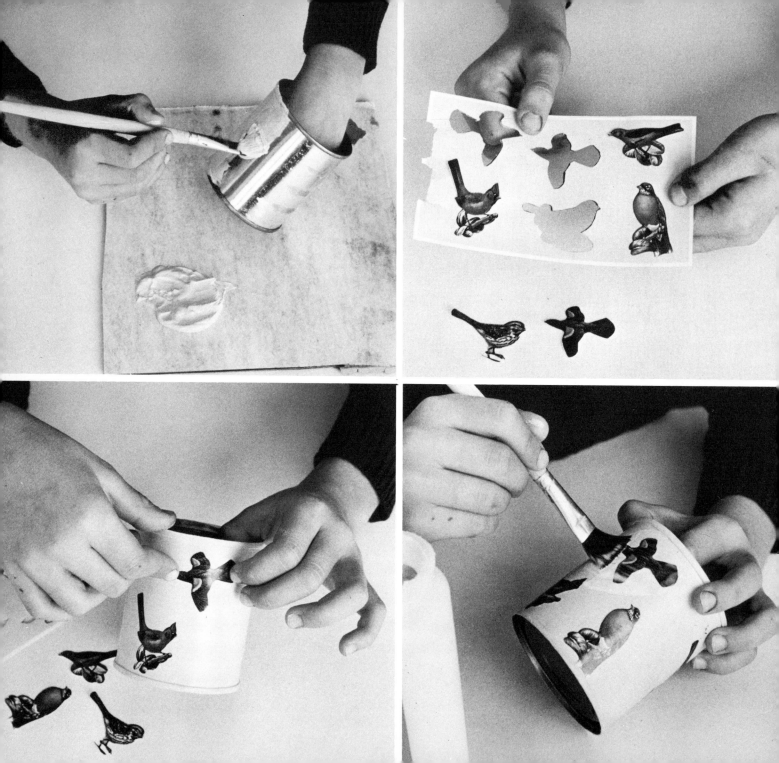

Peel the label off a clean, empty can. If you place one hand inside the can, you will be able to paint with the other. Paint it all the way around, but leave the bottom unpainted. Each of the children painted their cans a different color. One of the boys mixed gold and blue paint for a shimmery color. Try to do a neat painting job. If you place the can in a sunny place, it will dry in about 10 minutes. Wash your brush in warm water until all the paint is rinsed out of it.

Punch-out stickers are good to decorate your planter. You can buy them at the five-and-ten. Hardware stores also have decals that you can use. The children in this class were studying na-ture, so they used bird and leaf punch-out stick-ers. Punch them out with your finger. Then lick the back and place them on the can where you think they look best. Decide where you want to put the decorations before you lick them. One of the boys held his planter upside down to put the stickers on. All the birds were standing on their heads!

Press the stickers down with your hand so that they are in place. Use your clean brush to varnish all over the can and the designs. This will keep the paint from chipping and the designs from peel-ing off. It will also make your planter shiny. Put it aside to dry for 5 minutes.

15

When the planter is dry, fill it halfway with dirt or potting soil. Open your package of seeds and drop a few into the planter on top of the dirt. Spoon in more dirt on top of the seeds until the can is filled to the top. Pour a little bit of water—not too much—into the planter to wet the seeds. Now you must wait for your seeds to sprout.

When the dirt dries, water it again. Soon you will have a tiny garden right in your room. You can make several planters with different seeds in each.

When this project was finished, the boys and girls were proud of their decoupage planters. They had lots of ideas for decorating more cans at home.

Toy Tote

paper paint pail
paint
paintbrush (1″)
greeting cards, postcards,
    or magazines
small scissors
glue
varnish

Kate has lots of toys. She needs totes to hold everything. A toy tote made from a paper paint pail is good for this. You can buy these pails at the hardware store. There are big ones and medium-sized ones.

Kate used greeting cards for her designs. You could use postcards or magazines too.

First Kate painted the outside blue. After it dried, she painted the inside green. Remember to wash your brush after using each color paint. While the paint is drying, cut out the designs. This pail can have lots of different things on it.

Put some glue on the back of a picture and place it on the pail. Put one hand inside the pail and press the picture down with the other. Make sure the pictures are right side up and that all the edges are glued down well. When you have placed different designs all the way around the pail, you are ready to varnish. Check all the designs first

to be sure that they don't need more glue to hold them in place.

You could put your name around the top. Cut out letters from a magazine that spell your name. Plan where you will put each letter before gluing it in place. Gummed letters from the five-and-ten can be used for this.

Be sure that your brush is very clean before varnishing. Dip your brush into the varnish and brush it over the pail and pictures. This will protect your pail from dirt. It will also keep the pictures in place when you are using your tote.

When your tote is completely dry, you can fill it with toys.

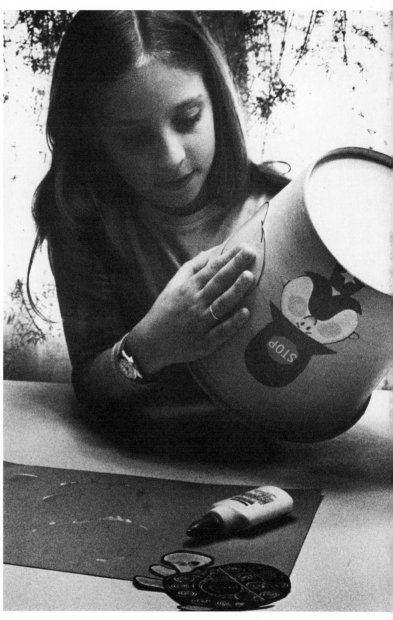

Pins and Barrettes

wrapping paper *or* decals
small scissors
glue
cardboard from shirt board
   or from a writing pad
pencil
small plastic *or* metal barrette
pin backing
clear nail polish

Making something to wear is a lot of fun. You can show it off right after you make it. If you have some friends over, you can work together. Most of the supplies you need for pins and barrettes are probably at home. The pin backings are from a hobby or craft shop. This is the part of the pin that attaches to your dress or shirt.

Choose pictures to cut out that are not too tiny. It is hard to cut out tiny things and they will not show up too well when you wear them.

Patty, Barbara, and Samantha used designs from wrapping paper and self-sticking hearts.

23

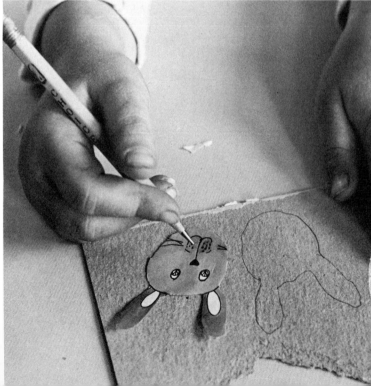

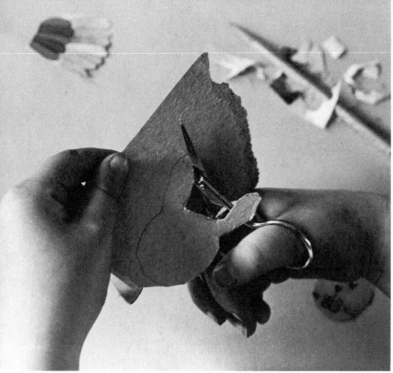

Pick out a picture that you like. Use a small scissors to cut as neatly as you can. Place the cutout picture on a piece of cardboard that is larger than the picture. Hold it there with your finger. Use a pencil to draw around the outside of the picture. This is called an outline. It doesn't have to be super neat. Take the picture away and cut out the piece of cardboard.

Now squirt a little glue right in the middle of the cutout cardboard piece. Smoosh it around with your finger. Wipe your finger off. Pick up the cutout picture. Lay it down on the glue so that it matches the cardboard shape. Press them together. This makes your picture stiff.

Turn the whole thing over so that the back of the cardboard is facing up. Squirt a few drops of glue in the middle of the cardboard back. Take your pin backing or your barrette (whichever one you are making) and press it onto the glue. Now let it dry for about 10 minutes.

Then turn the pin back or barrette over so you can see the picture. Wipe off any extra glue with a wet sponge. Use clear nail polish as varnish and carefully spread it over the front of the picture with the nail polish brush. The picture will be shiny. It will take about 5 minutes for the nail polish to dry.

When it is dry, turn the picture over. Put some polish all over the back on the cardboard. Let this dry. If you polish the front again, this will make it stiffer and shinier. Let it dry again. Blow on it to speed up the drying. Now you can wear it. If you have made a pin, you can pin it to the curtain in your room when you're not wearing it.

Whenever you want something new to wear, you can make a pin or decorate a barrette. Keep the scraps to use again. When you have a friend visiting, you can do this project together.

Hand Mirror

paddle-ball toy
small piece of fine sandpaper
paint
paintbrush (½″ or ¾″)
wax paper
round mirror, about 3″ diameter
glue

small scissors
construction paper
pencil
ruler
self-sticking dot labels
gummed gold letters (optional)
varnish

The hand mirror is made from a paddle-ball toy. If you don't have one you can get it in the five-and-ten. Cut the ball and elastic string off the paddle part. Use a blunt knife to remove the staple. Now you have a piece of wood that is the perfect size and shape for a hand mirror.

Hand mirrors look pretty on a dresser when you aren't using them. They are nice for looking at yourself close up.

29

Sometimes the paddle is made of rough wood. When you pick it up, be careful not to get a splinter. Use a small piece of fine sandpaper to smooth the edges and the front and back of the paddle. It is best to do sanding outside. If you do it inside, put paper on the floor under your work area. You won't have to sand it too much. Just make it a little bit smoother. Blow on the paddle to get all the "sand dust" off. Now you are ready to paint.

Cathy used bright yellow paint for the mirror side and a golden yellow for the edges and the back. You should make yours just the way you want it to look. Maybe you'd like to have it match the curtains or bedspread in your room. You won't need much space. Cathy worked at the small desk in her room.

Paint the paddle as neatly as possible. If you lay the paddle down on wax paper, you can paint the front and let it dry without sticking.

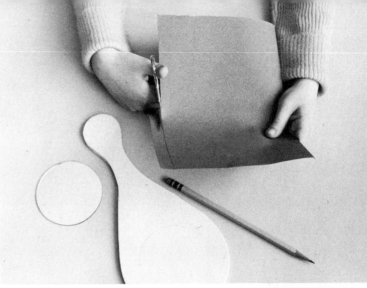

While you are waiting for the paint to dry on the front, put your brush in a cup of warm water. This will keep it soft. Then paint the back. Wash your brush again. When the paddle is very dry, place the mirror in the middle of the top part. Draw a circle around it with your pencil. Take the mirror away.

Before Cathy glued the mirror in place, she made a skinny green stem for the flower design. Here's how to do it. Put your piece of construction paper next to the paddle. Draw a line half an inch in from the edge of the paper. Use a ruler to measure and to make a straight line. Cut along the line for a stem that is 8 inches long. Draw two leaves on the paper and cut them out. This isn't hard to do. Leaves come in all shapes. You can cut them any way you want. Look at the photo at the right to see how Cathy made her leaves. Set these pieces aside.

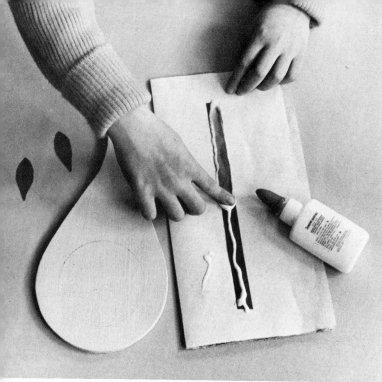

Turn the stem over and put a little glue on the back. Smoosh it with your finger. Carefully lift the stem. Place the bottom of the stem at the edge of the paddle handle. Lay the rest of the stem down. Try to keep it going straight up the handle in the center of the paddle. It should go inside of the mirror circle that you drew.

Press it down with your hand. Pat it with a damp sponge to pick up any extra glue. Now put glue on the back of each leaf. Put the leaves down near the stem where you think they will look best.

Open your box of self-sticking dots. Use any color you like. Cathy chose bright orange.

Place the first dot down so that it goes a little over the mirror pencil line. This is the first petal

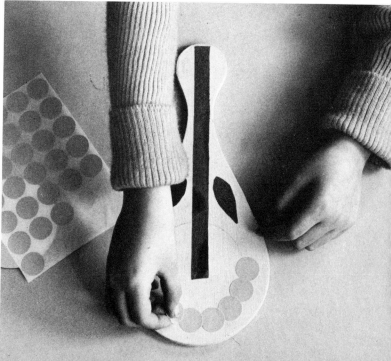

of the flower. Place another dot on the paddle so that it covers the first one a tiny bit. Keep adding dots all the way around the circle.

Turn the mirror over and squirt glue all over the back. Spread it with your finger. Carefully lift the mirror by the edges and place it on the paddle so it covers part of the dots. Then let the mirror dry in place. Do not lift the mirror up for at least 10 minutes. If it isn't dry, the mirror will slide off when you lift it because it's heavy.

Dip your clean brush into the varnish. Spread the varnish over the paddle, the petals, leaves and stem, but NOT the mirror. Let the varnish dry for 5 minutes. Apply another coat of varnish and let it dry well.

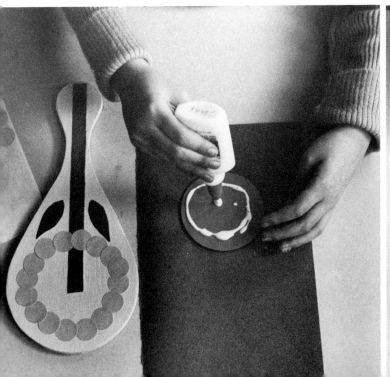

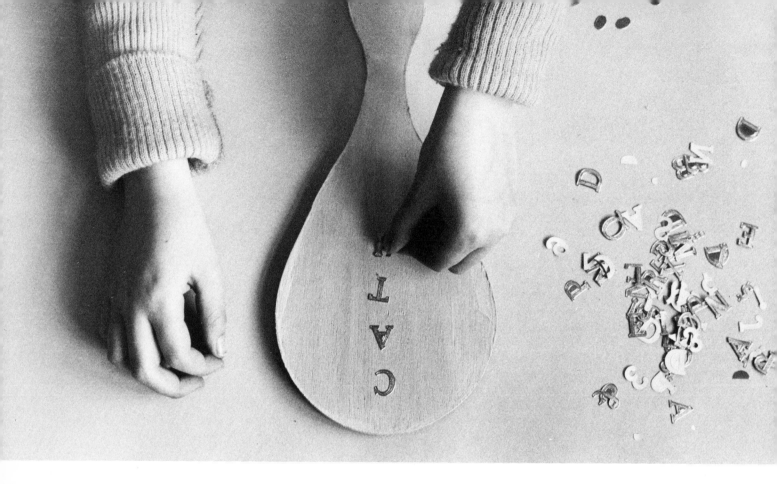

Now you can decorate the back of the mirror. If you want to spell your name, use a package of gummed gold letters from the five-and-ten. Line them up in the right order before you lick the back of each letter and place it in a nice design on the paddle. The letters can go down the middle of the paddle like Cathy's. They can go straight across. Or they can be placed in a crazy pattern. Brush a coat of varnish all over this side of the paddle. Let it dry for 10 minutes and you are done.

Some other time you might like to make this again with another design. Instead of using the dots for petals, you could use a paper doily that is larger than the mirror. You glue a doily to the paddle. Then place the mirror in the center of the doily and you have a lacy kind of flower.

You can have a lot of fun thinking up new ways to do this project. Cathy said that she is going to teach everyone to make this mirror at her next Brownie meeting.

Wall Plaque and Key Holder

wooden board
   plaque (6″ x 9″)
   key holder (4″ x 6″)
sandpaper
paint *or* wood stain
paintbrush (½″ to 1″)
varnish

rub-on transfer design
ruler
pencil
hammer
nail
brass screw ring
L hooks *or* cup hooks

You can make a plaque to hang in your room or give as a present. Maybe you'd like to have a key holder to hang on the wall. Both of these projects are made by using a precut wooden board that you can buy in a craft or hobby store. If you have a piece of wood at home that you think is a good size, use it. The rub-on transfers are like decals and most craft stores have them. They are fun to use. You do not have to cut out the pictures or lick the glue. Just rub them on the board and lift off the wax paper backing.

    Anthony is ten. He wanted to make something for a wall in his room. He also wanted to make a present for his father. He decided to make a wall plaque first. It was a nice day for working outside and all his friends came around to see what he was doing.

37

Anthony's plaque is 6 by 9 inches. The key holder that he made is 4 by 6 inches. Use the size that works best for your design.

To make either one of these projects, begin by sanding the wood to make it smooth. Blow off the "sand dust." Next paint the front and sides but not the back. Anthony painted his plaque blue. It is a good color for the ship design he chose. If you have some wood stain, you can stain the board instead of painting it. Brush the stain on with the paintbrush and the wood turns brown. Stain takes longer to dry than paint. Be sure to let it dry very well.

While Anthony was painting, his little sister Senta was trying to sneak up behind him. He knew she was there, but he pretended not to see her. When the plaque was painted, he put it on the rock to dry. His dog came running over to greet him and ran right over the plaque. Anthony had to paint it again.

When your plaque is dry, place the rub-on design where you want it to go. Use the handle of your brush to rub over the picture.

Then lift off the backing and, like magic, the design is stuck to the board. If you don't have rub-on transfers, cut out a picture from a magazine and glue it in place. Keep adding designs wherever you think they will look nice.

With a ruler, measure across the top of the board. Make a pencil mark at the center of the top edge. Use your hammer and nail to tap a small hole in the top where you made the mark. Pull the nail out and screw the brass ring into the top. This ring is used to hang your plaque on the wall.

Brush a coat of varnish over the plaque to protect the picture and make it shiny. Let the varnish dry for about 5 minutes.

Key Holder

To make a key holder, first sand and then paint or stain the board the same way you would for a wall plaque. Before you put your design in place, plan where you will put the hooks for the keys. The design should show when the keys are hanging up. To work this out, place the keys on the board. Then use a pencil to mark the holes for the hooks.

Now you are ready to lay the design in place. With the brush handle, rub the design down so that it sticks to the board. Lift the backing off the design.

By the time Anthony was this far along, he let Senta watch. She promised not to touch.

Use a nail to make small holes where you will screw in the hooks. Tap the nail in lightly with your hammer. Then pull the nail out. Anthony made three holes to hold the hooks for three keys.

Leave spaces between the hooks. Then twist the L screws or cup hooks into the tiny holes that you made. With a ruler, measure across the top to make a hole so you can screw the brass ring into the middle.

Last of all, you can brush a coat of varnish over the key holder. This will keep it protected from scratch marks. Let the varnish dry for about 5 minutes. Then you can wrap it up to give as a gift or use it yourself.

Collector's Box

oatmeal box
wrapping paper
cup *or* water glass
glue
large scissors
pencil
varnish
paintbrush (1")

If you collect things, you need a box to store your collections. A decoupaged box may be just right. You can then keep the box on a shelf where it will look nice. Richard made a box for his pebble collection. If you wear ribbons, you might like to make a ribbon box. Look for wrapping paper that you like.

45

Save an empty oatmeal box or put the cereal in a large jar or can. Peel as much of the label off the box as you can. Lay the empty oatmeal box down at the edge of your wrapping paper. The paper should be 3 inches longer than the box, 1½ inches at the top and 1½ inches at the bottom.

Hold one end of the paper on the box and roll the paper around it. Make a pencil mark on the paper where you will cut it. Leave a little extra to overlap the edge of the paper when it is rolled around the box. Using the scissors, cut off the extra paper where you've made the mark.

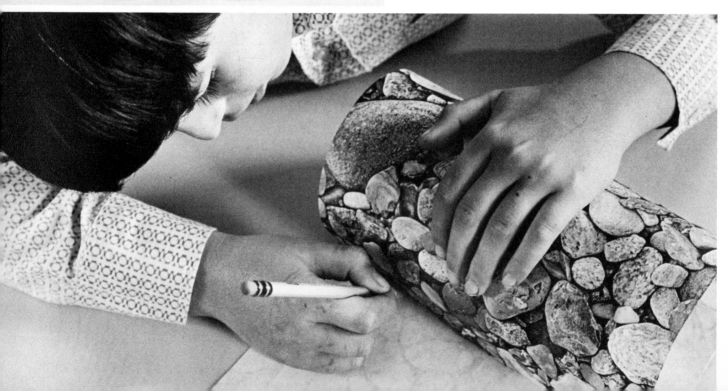

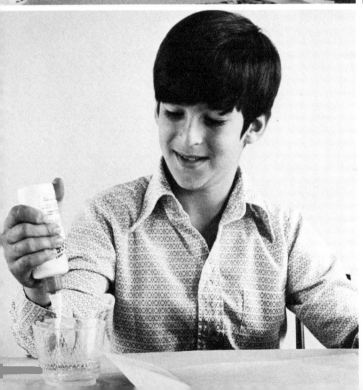

Put 1 large spoonful of water in a cup. Squirt about 2 spoonfuls of glue into the cup with the water. Take your brush and mix up the glue and the water. Now brush the glue mixture all over the outside of the box.

Be sure that you coat the entire box with glue. If some parts dry while you are doing this, brush more glue over the box. If it doesn't feel sticky enough, put a few more drops of glue into the water cup and mix it around. The box should be very wet so that the paper sticks.

47

Before the glue dries, place your box at one edge of the paper. Be sure the extra paper shows at the top and bottom. Hold tightly to the other end of the paper. Roll the box slowly over the paper. If you do this carefully, the paper will be smoothly glued around the box. Smooth it over the box as you roll it.

Now brush glue on the bottom of the box. Tuck the extra 1½ inches of paper under the bottom, pinching the paper in a few spots to fit. Brush the glue mix on the inside of the box. Fold the extra paper over the top and tuck it inside the box. Pinch the paper in a few spots and press it against the inside walls of the box.

Use a smaller piece of paper to cover the box top. Place the top on the paper. Draw a circle around the top on the paper so it is about 1 inch larger all around the top. Put glue on the box top and sides. Place the top in the center of the paper. Press the paper up onto the sides of the top. Now brush glue on the inside edge of the box top. Press the paper on the inside, pinching it in a few spots. This will dry quickly.

Wash your brush and cup out in clear warm water.

Dip your brush into the varnish. Paint the whole box with varnish. Do the inside and the top too. When this dries it will be stiff and shiny. Make sure the varnish dries completely so that the top won't stick to the box. You can varnish it again when it is dry. The box is finished when the varnish doesn't feel sticky. If the box top sticks, rub a bit of soap on the inside edge. Now you can go collecting.

If you don't have an oatmeal box, you can do this project with a large coffee can that has a plastic lid. Do not cover the lid with paper. You could cut out a design and glue it to the top and then varnish the design.

Card Caddy

Sucret tin
tiny playing cards *or* school photo
glue
paint
paintbrush (¼″ to ½″)
varnish
Contact *or* wrapping paper
pencil
scissors

Sucret tins are excellent for craft projects. A package of miniature playing cards can fit into one or the tins can be used to hold pushpins or paper clips. They are also the right size to hold small pieces of jewelry.

Jennie painted her card caddy sky blue and decorated it with three cards.

51

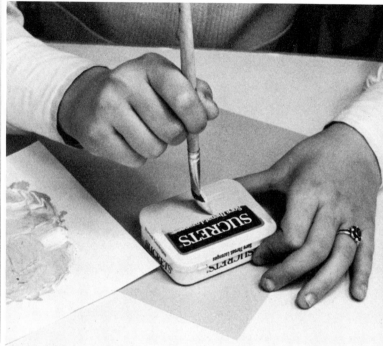

First paint the tin. Put it on a windowsill in the sun to speed up the drying. It should take about 10 minutes. You may need a second coat of paint.

Choose the cards you want to use for the top. Spread glue over the back of one card. Lay it at a slant on the top of the tin. Put some glue on another card and place it so that it overlaps the first card a little bit. You should have room for one more card on top of the tin. If some of the glue

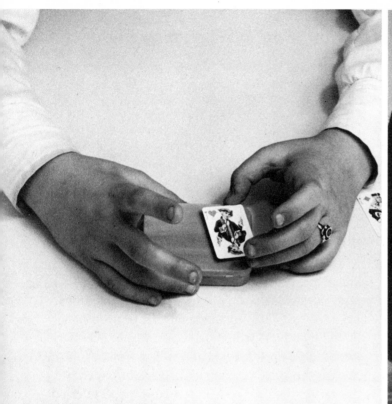

oozes out from under the cards, pat it up with a damp sponge or paper towel. Let the cards dry for a few minutes. Cards take longer than thin paper to dry.

While they are drying, you can get ready to line the box. Lining the box with Contact or wrapping paper is a nice extra touch. It will be a real surprise when you open it to show someone. Jennie lined hers with yellow paper.

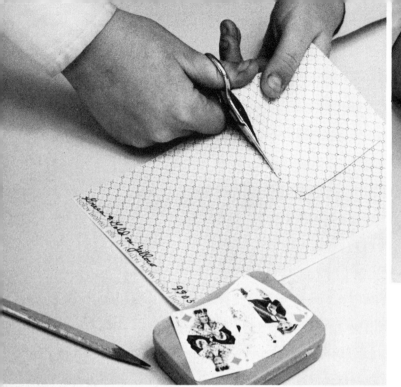

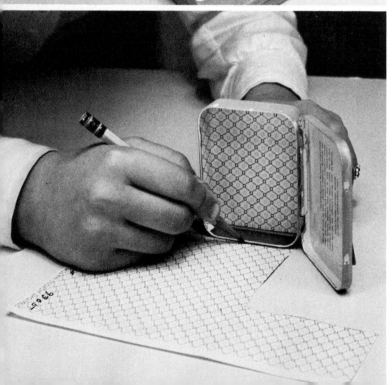

You can line the inside bottom, front, and back. Place the box in a corner of the paper. With a pencil draw a line on the paper around the box. Take the box off the paper and cut out the paper shape. If you use wrapping paper, turn it over and spread glue on the back. If you use Contact, just peel off the backing. Place this piece of paper into the bottom of the box. Part of the paper should go up the sides of the front and back. Press the paper in place.

Now stand the tin on its side on the paper. Draw a line around one side of the tin. Cut this out. Do it again for the other side. If you are using wrapping paper, turn these pieces over and put glue on the backs. Place one on each side of the inside bottom. This will finish the lining for the bottom. Then you can cut a piece to fit the inside of the top.

Using the varnish, coat the outside of the tin

right over the cards. Do the sides and back of the outside. Let this dry with the top open for about 10 minutes. Then brush the varnish over the inside right on top of the paper. This will make it shiny and keep it from ripping or coming off. Make sure the varnish dries very well so that the cover hinge does not stick. Then varnish the bottom.

If lining the box seems too hard for you to do, you can paint the inside instead. Try using a different color from the one used on the outside of the box.

You can also decoupage this tin with a small photo. Glue it to the top. Then cut out designs from wrapping paper to add around the photo. You could cut out butterflies and add a flower for another type of design, as Jennie did. This can be a jewelry box. Her box is painted yellow and the butterflies are pink. Do the project that you like best or make up your own design.

Thank You

This book was a lot of fun to do because the boys and girls who did the projects were fun to know. They made helpful suggestions. Since they did all the projects, they could tell me which they liked best. Because of this, I could write the directions in the easiest way for you to follow. I hope you enjoyed doing decoupage with: Douglas and Rebecca Ellsley, Samantha Rochlin, Kate Allen, Barbara and Patty Gross, Cathy Kastriner, Anthony Huggins, Richard Gross, Jennie Allen, and the third-grade class of planter makers: Tim Prins, Dargie Gillett, Ted Coine, Eric Wern, Mike Herman, Erin Cooper, Carey Sterling, and Eve Schmitt.

—Leslie Linsley